Anthology of Alternative Rock

This publication is not for sale in the E.C. and/or Australia or New Zealand.

ISBN 0-7935-5251-6

HAL•LEONARD® CORPORATION
7777 W. BLUEMOUND RD. P.O. BOX 13819 MILWAUKEE, WI 53213

Copyright © 1996 by HAL LEONARD CORPORATION
International Copyright Secured   All Rights Reserved

For all works contained herein:
Unauthorized copying, arranging, adapting, recording or public performance is an infringement of copyright.
Infringers are liable under the law.

Visit Hal Leonard on the internet at http://www.halleonard.com

Anthology of Alternative Rock

Contents

Are You Gonna Go My Way · · · 4
LENNY KRAVITZ

Awake · · · · · · · · · · · · · 9
LETTERS TO CLEO

Black Hole Sun · · · · · · · · 14
SOUNDGARDEN

Blood and Roses · · · · · · · 19
SMITHEREENS

Cumbersome · · · · · · · · · 22
SEVEN MARY THREE

Danny Boy · · · · · · · · · · 28
BLACK 47

Ecstasy · · · · · · · · · · · · 36
RUSTED ROOT

Feed the Tree · · · · · · · · · 44
BELLY

God Shuffled His Feet · · · · 50
CRASH TEST DUMMIES

Good Enough · · · · · · · · · 56
SARAH McLACHLAN

The Great Big No · · · · · · · 61
LEMONHEADS

Hand in My Pocket · · · · · · · 66
ALANIS MORISSETTE

Hold Me, Thrill Me, Kiss Me,
Kill Me · · · · · · · · · · · · · 70
U2

I'll Stick Around · · · · · · · 76
FOO FIGHTERS

Let Her Cry · · · · · · · · · · 90
HOOTIE & THE BLOWFISH

Man in the Box · · · · · · · · 94
ALICE IN CHAINS

Man on the Moon · · · · · · · 98
R.E.M.

Molly (Sixteen Candles) · · 83
SPONGE

Name · · · · · · · · · · · · · 105
GOO GOO DOLLS

Nearly Lost You · · · · · · · 112
SCREAMING TREES

Ode to My Family · · · · · · 118
THE CRANBERRIES

Right Here, Right Now · · · 139
JESUS JONES

Scum · · · · · · · · · · · · · 124
MEAT PUPPETS

Sick of Myself · · · · · · · · 128
MATTHEW SWEET

Stars · · · · · · · · · · · · · 132
HUM

Starseed · · · · · · · · · · · 144
OUR LADY PEACE

Stutter · · · · · · · · · · · · 152
ELASTICA

Supernova · · · · · · · · · · 156
LIZ PHAIR

Trigger Happy Jack · · · · · 159
(Drive By a Go-Go)
POE

Two Princes · · · · · · · · · 164
SPIN DOCTORS

Under the Bridge · · · · · · 186
RED HOT CHILI PEPPERS

Undone - The Sweater Song · · 170
WEEZER

What's Up · · · · · · · · · · 174
4 NON BLONDES

Wonderwall · · · · · · · · · 180
OASIS

ARE YOU GONNA GO MY WAY

Words by LENNY KRAVITZ
Music by LENNY KRAVITZ
and CRAIG ROSS

Medium fast
N.C.

Play 4 times

E5   Play 4 times   E5

I was born
I don't know why

long a-go;   I am the cho-sen, I'm the one.
we al-ways cry,   this we must leave and get un-done.

I have come   to save the day,   and I won't leave un-til I'm
We must en-gage   and re-ar-range   and turn this plan-et back to

Copyright © 1993 Miss Bessie Music (ASCAP) and Wigged Music (BMI)
International Copyright Secured   All Rights Reserved

done.
one.

G5

So that's why you've got to try,
So tell me why we've got to die

you've got to breathe and have some fun.
and kill each oth-er one by one.

E5

Though I'm not paid, I play this game,
We've got to love and rub-a-dub,

and I won't stop un-til I'm done.
we've got to dance and be in love.

G6

But what I real-ly

want to know is: Are you gonna go my way? And I got to, got to know.

to know.

Play 4 times

Play 7 times

E5
G6
Play 4 times
F♯m7
G6
F♯m7
E
D
E
G6
F♯m7
Are you gon-na go my way?
'Cause ba-by, I
E5
got to know.

AWAKE

Words and Music by GREG McKENNA, STACY JONES,
SCOTT RIEBLING, KAY HANLEY and MICHAEL EISENSTEIN

Moderate Rock

I guess it's been a while
I wash my hands of you.
and a long time too.
I wash my dirty feet too.
Ev-'ry-thing's still the same and so are you.
And when I wash my hair the dust clouds dis-ap-pear.

Copyright © 1995 by Rebecca Lula Music and Famous Music Corporation
International Copyright Secured   All Rights Reserved

It's on - ly in this light that I could see
You're lean - ing out the win - dow you're beat - ing down
I wish we had a laugh, but you're just

what you'd be like. If it took a mil - lion years, well
a path real slow with your heav - y plas - tic bags and
not fun - ny. Ba - by, I'm leav - ing out the

this is what I am.
heav - y head.
i - ro - ny.

You're a - wake and
I'm a - sleep and we are so com - plete that way.

A B E G♯ D A/C♯ B
You're a-sleep and I'm a-wake and ev-'ry-thing's so great.
D F♯m7 B
1
E G♯+ A
Ev-'ry-thing is so great. Oh, yeah.
E G♯+ A A/B
2
D A/C♯ B
Heav - y. great, yeah.
C♯m D E B

12

CODA

You're a-wake and I'm a-sleep and we are so complete that way. You're a-sleep and I'm a-wake and ev-'ry-thing's so great, oh yeah. ev-'ry-thing's so great. Ev-'ry-thing is so great, yeah.

BLACK HOLE SUN

Words and Music by
CHRIS CORNELL

Slow Rock

In my eyes, in-dis-posed, in-dis-
ing, cold and damp. Steal the

guise as no one knows, hides the face, lies the snake, and the
warm wind ti-red friend. Times are gone for hon-est men, and some-times

sun in my dis-grace. Boil-ing heat, sum-mer stretch. 'Neath the
far too long for snakes. In my shoes, a walk-ing sleep, and my

Copyright © 1994 You Make Me Sick I Make Music (ASCAP)
International Copyright Secured All Rights Reserved

black, the sky looks dead. Call me name through the cream, and I'll
youth I pray to keep. Heav-en send hell a-way. No one
hear you scream a-gain.
sings like you an-y-more. Black hole sun, won't you come and
wash a-way the rain? Black hole sun, won't you come? Won't you come?

1. Won't you come? Stut-ter -
2. Black hole

sun, won't you come __ and wash a-way __ the rain? __ Black hole

sun, won't you come? __ Won't you come? __

Won't you come? __

Won't you come? __

17

Won't you come?

Won't you come?

Won't you come?

BLOOD AND ROSES

Words and Music by
PAT DiNIZIO

Medium Rock

(1.,D.S.) It was long ago. It seems like yesterday. Saw you standin' in the rain, then I heard you say:

(2.) flowers in the springtime, October we were wed. The wintertime the roses died, the blood ran cold and then she said: "I

© 1986 EMI BLACKWOOD MUSIC INC.
All Rights Reserved   International Copyright Secured   Used by Permission

20

21

CUMBERSOME

Words and Music by JASON ROSS
and JASON POLLOCK

Moderate Rock (not too fast)

She calls me Go-li-ath and I wear the Da-vid mask.
I'd like to be-lieve we could re-con-cile the past,

I guess the stones are com-ing too fast for her now.
res-ur-rect those bridg-es with an an-cient glance.

© 1995 EMI BLACKWOOD MUSIC INC. and SEVEN MARY THREE MUSIC
All Rights Controlled and Administered by EMI BLACKWOOD MUSIC INC.
All Rights Reserved   International Copyright Secured   Used by Permission

You know I'd like to be-lieve this ner-vous-ness will pass.
But my old stone face can't seem to break her down.

All the stones that are thrown are build-ing up a wall.
She re-mem-bers bridg-es, burns 'em to the ground.

I have be-come cum-ber-some to this world.

I have become _____ cum - ber - some _____ to my girl. _____

Too heav-y, too light, too black or too white, too wrong or too right, to-day or to-nite, _____ cum - ber - some. _____

Too rich or too poor, she's wanting me less and I'm wanting her more.

The bitter taste is cumbersome. No, yeah.

No, no, no.

No, no, no, yeah.

There is __ a balance between two worlds, __ one with an arrow and __ a cross. __ Regardless of the balance, life has become cumbersome.

D.S. al Coda

CODA

No, — yeah. No, no, no. —

No, no, no, — yeah. —

No, no, no, — no, —

yeah. _____ Your — life has be-come cum-ber-some.

DANNY BOY

Words and Music by
LARRY KIRWAN

Moderate Chorale style

Moderate Hip-Hop Rock

© 1994 EMI BLACKWOOD MUSIC INC. and STARRY PLOUGH MUSIC
All Rights Controlled and Administered by EMI BLACKWOOD MUSIC INC.
All Rights Reserved   International Copyright Secured   Used by Permission

Rap: 1. Danny came over to old New York from Bandon town in county Cork. He got a room on the avenue in Woodside Queens
2., 3. *(See additional lyrics)*

and a job off books doin' demolition. He was kind of diff'rent than ev'ryone else oh he liked to hang out all by himself. Didn't hit

those bars in Sunnyside Queens went straight into the village to check out the scene.

2. One

(Sung:) Then he met a man down in Sher-i-dan Square. They moved in to-geth-er for a cou-ple of years. Said it was the hap-pi-est he'd ev-er been do-in' what he want-ed liv-in' his dream. We used to drink to-geth-er down on Av-e-nue B.

One gray dawn he confessed to me "Love's the only thing that makes the world go 'round and I'm never gonna see another sunset over sweet Bandon town."

D.S. al Coda

CODA

(Spoken:) "life's a bitch and then you die. (Sung:) Oh Danny boy the

freely *a tempo*

pipes the pipes are call-ing from glen to glen and down the moun-tain side. The sum-mer's gone and all the flowers are dy-in', 'tis you 'tis you must go and I must bide. But come you back when sum-mer's in the mead-ow or when the val-ley's hushed and white with snow. 'Tis I'll be there in

Additional Lyrics

2. One day on the job the foreman said
   "Hey Danny Boy we think you're a fag
   With your ponytail and that ring in your ear
   Hey, we don't need no homos foulin' up the air"
   Danny just smiled and picked up a 2 by 4
   He split that jerk from his jaw to his ear
   Said "You can stick your job where the sun don't shine
   [But you're] never gonna stop me bein' what I am, boy!"

3. Last time I saw Dan he was in a hospital bed
   Two tubes hangin' out the nose of his head
   He smiled at me with them stone blue eyes
   And he said, "Hey, how you doin', guy?
   I'm history 'round here in a couple of weeks
   I did what I wanted - I got no regrets
   So, when you think of me crack a beer and smile
   Hey, life's a bitch and then you die."

ECSTASY

Words and Music by MIKE GLABICKI,
JIM DONOVAN, JENN WERTZ, LIZ BERLIN,
JIM DI SPIRITO, JOHN BUYNAK and PATRICK NORMAN

Moderately fast

Tak-in' a-way your pa-per and pen, __ stacks of mo-ney and your
Take a-way your com-pan-ies. __ Take a-way your so-

fool-ish grin, __ and go.
ci-e-ties __ and go.

Get me off the
Get me off this

Copyright © 1995 PolyGram International Publishing, Inc. and Rusted Root Publishing, Inc.
International Copyright Secured   All Rights Reserved

back - wards ride. Take a - way your greed - y way and
back - wards ride. Take a - way your fic - tion books of

go.
fact.

See the wom - an stand - ing in the door. World gone by,
a-gain and a - gain.

See the blis - ters grow-ing on your feet.

Pushed on, pushed on.

Ooh, the world gone by.

Em
1
Dm
Ooh, the world gone by.
2
Dm
Em
Ooh, the world gone by.
Dm
Em
Ooh, the world gone by.
Dm
I would-n't want to be

living in a world of ecstasy ____ with ____ you.

I would-n't want to be ____ living in a world of ecstasy ____ with ____ you.

To Coda ⊕

Was-ted arms, was-ted legs, wrapped 'round this ma-chine. The mil-i-ta-ry ma-

chine; the mil-i-ta-ry ma-

chine. Ooh, the mil-i-ta-ry,

ooh, the mil-i-ta-ry ma-chine. Ooh, the

B♭
C
mil - i - ta - ry, ooh, the mil - i - ta - ry ma -
D
D.S. al Coda
chine.
CODA
G
Dm
3
Dm(add2)
Dm
Dm(add2)
Dm

FEED THE TREE

Words and Music by
TANYA DONELLY

Moderately

This old man I've talked about broke his own heart, poured it in the ground.
This lit-tle squirrel I used to be slammed her bike down the stairs.
This old man I used to be spins a-round, a-round, a-round the tree.

A

Vocal line written one octave higher than sung.

Copyright © 1993 Songs Of PolyGram International, Inc., Mercer Street Songs and Slow Dog Music
International Copyright Secured   All Rights Reserved

big red tree grew up and out,_ throws up its leaves,_ spins
They put sil-ver where her teeth had been. Ba-by sil-ver tooth,_ she
Sil-ver ba-by, come to me. I'll on-ly hurt you

'round and 'round.
grins and grins.
in my dreams.

I know

all of this_ and more._ So, take your

hat {off / off, boy} when you're talk-ing to me — and be — there when I feed the tree.

Take your hat off, boy when you're talk-ing to me — and be —

there when I feed the tree.

CODA

all of this and I know all of this and I know all of this and more.

So, take you're hat off, boy when you're talk-ing to me and be
hat off when you're talk-ing to me and be

there when I feed the tree.
there when I feed the tree.

49

Take your

God Shuffled His Feet

Words and Music by
BRAD ROBERTS

Moderately
no chord

After seven days, He was quite tired, so God said: "Let there be a

Copyright © 1993 PolyGram International Publishing, Inc., Door Number Two Music and Dummies Productions, Inc.
International Copyright Secured   All Rights Reserved

day — just for pic-nics, with wine and bread."

He gath-ered up some peo-ple He had made, Cre-at-ed blan-kets and laid back in the shade.

The peo - ple sipped their wine, and what with God there, they asked Him with
"Once there was a boy who woke up out on their blan - kets in the
peo - ple sat wait-ing

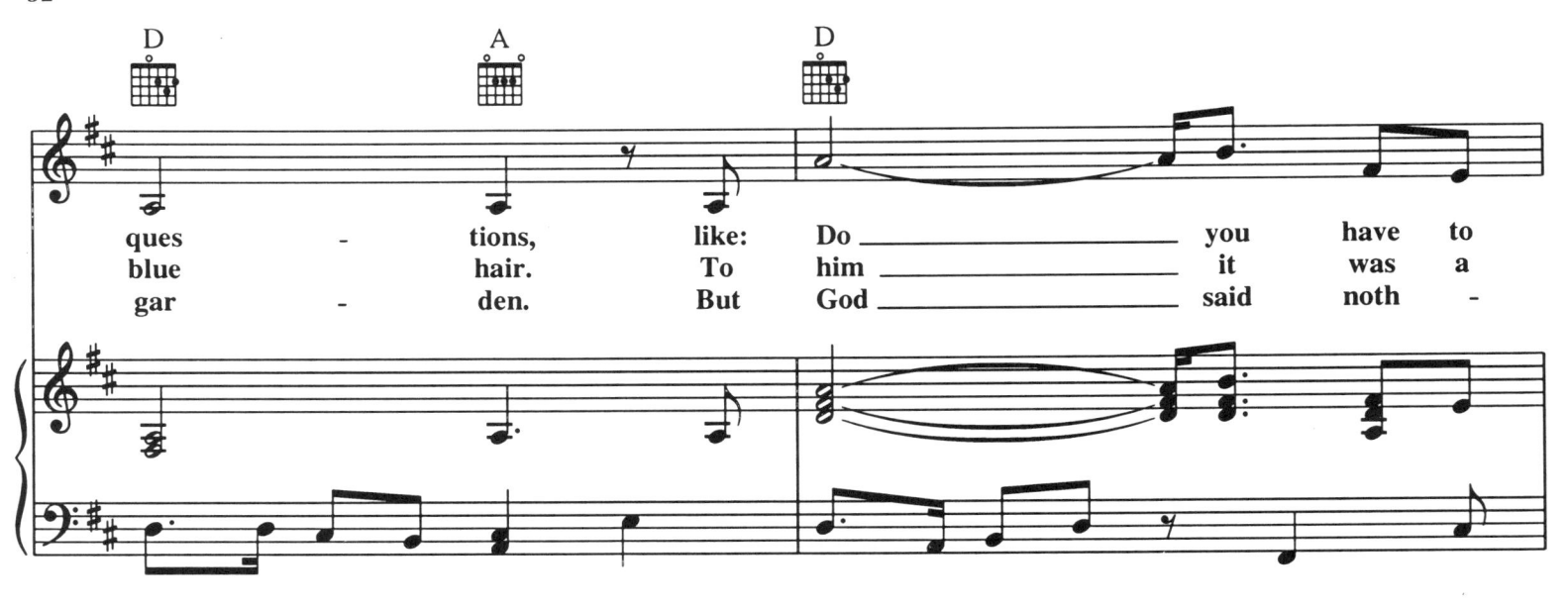

ques - tions, like: Do ____ you have to
blue hair. To him ____ it was a
gar - den. But God ____ said noth -

eat __ or get your hair cut in
joy, __ un - til he ran out in - to the
ing. __ So, some - one asked Him, "I beg your

heav - en? ____ And if your eye __ got
warm air. ____ He thought of how __ his
par - don: ____ I'm not quite clear __ a -

poked out in this life, would it be wait-ing up ___ in
friends would come to see; and would they laugh or had ___ he
bout what you just spoke. Was that a par-a-ble ___ or a

heav-en with your wife?)
got some strange dis-ease?" } God ___ shuf-fled His
ver-y sub-tle ___ joke?"}

feet and glanced a-round at them. The

peo - ple cleared their ___ throats and stared right ___

back at Him. So, He said:

The

55

GOOD ENOUGH

Words and Music by
SARAH McLACHLAN

Hey, your glass is emp-ty; it's a hell of a long way home.
Hey, lit-tle girl, would you like some can-dy? Your mom-ma said that it's o-kay.

Why don't you let me take you; it's no
The door is o-pen, come on out-side. No, I

Copyright © 1993 Sony/ATV Songs LLC and Tyde Music
All Rights Administered by Sony/ATV Music Publishing, 8 Music Square West, Nashville, TN 37203
International Copyright Secured   All Rights Reserved

good to go __ a - lone. __ I nev-er would have o-
can't come out __ to - day. It's not the wind that cracked __

-pened __ up, but you seemed so real __ to me.
your __ shoul - der and threw you to __ the ground.

Af - ter all the bull - shit I've __ heard, it's re - fresh-ing not __ to see.
Who's there that makes you so __ a - fraid. __ You're shak-en to __ the bone.

I don't have to pre-tend; she does-n't ex - pect __ it from
You know I don't un - der - stand; you de-serve so much more than this.

Chorus
A
A7sus
A
D
me.
Don't tell me I have-n't been good
So, don't tell me why he's nev-er been good
F♯m
D
F♯m
to you. Don't tell me I have-n't been there for you. Just tell me why
to you. Don't tell me why he's nev-er been there for you. And I'll tell you that
D
A
E
1
why noth-ing is good e-nough.
is sim-ply not good e-nough.
2
Esus
E
D
F♯m
Oh, so just let me try and I will be good to you. Just let me try

and I will be there _ for _ you. I'll show you why _ you're so much more than good e-nough.

Guitar solo

So, don't tell me why ___ he's nev-er been good to you. Don't tell me why ___
and I will be good to you. Just let me try ___

he's nev-er been there ___ for you. And I'll tell you that why ___ is sim-ply not
and I will be there ___ for you. I'll show you why ___ you're so much more ___ than

good e-nough.
good e-nough. Oh, so just let me try ___

Repeat ad lib. and Fade

THE GREAT BIG NO

Words and Music by TOM MORGAN
and EVAN DANDO

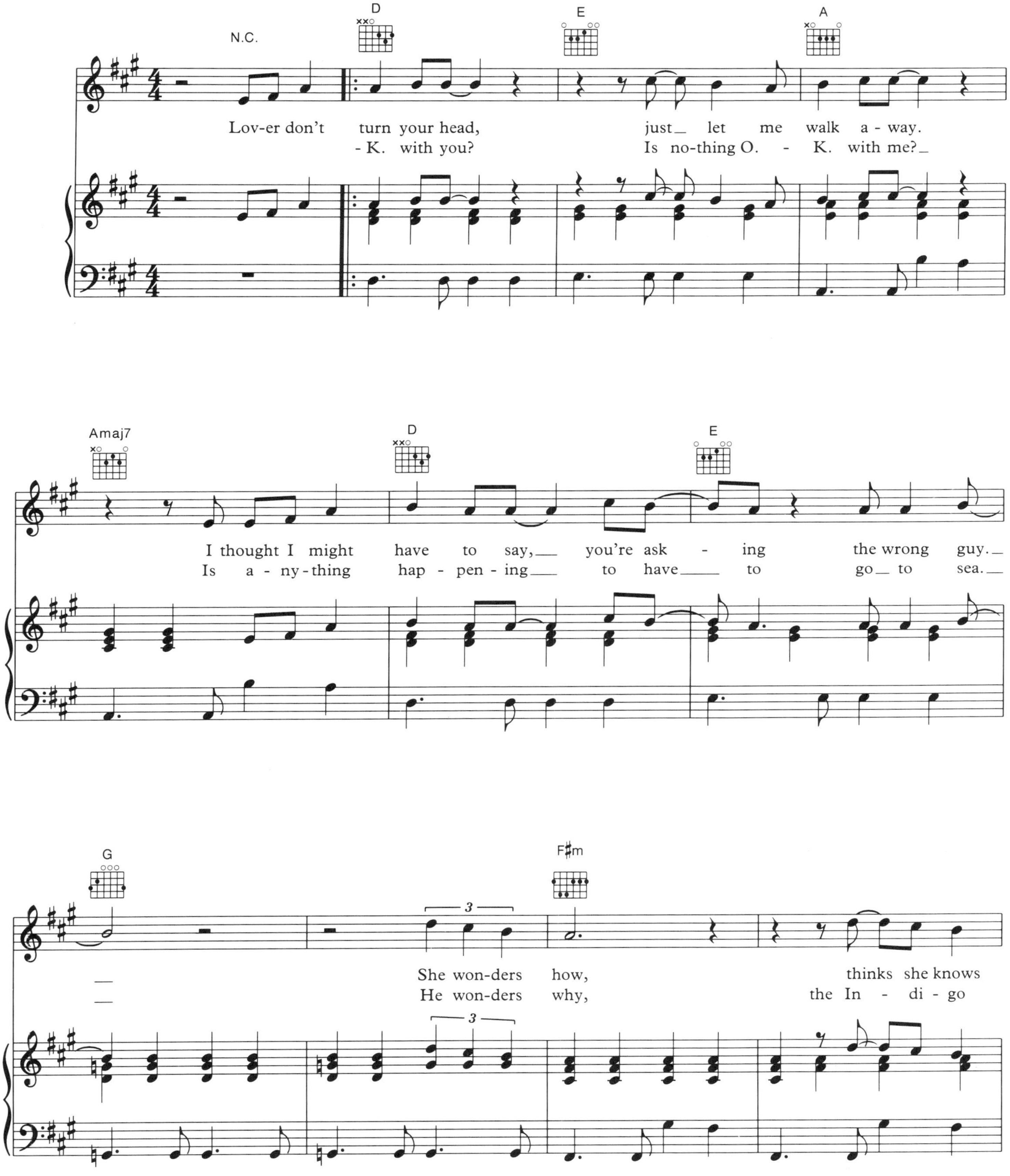

D
E
D
E
now, she'll be right, they al - ways go
Guy, he'll be right,
D
E
D
bye the bye. The great big
A/D
D
no, the great big no, the great big
1.
A/D
D
no, the great big no.

E
A
Amaj7
D
E
A
N.C.
Is no-thing O. -
2.
A/D
Bm
F♯m
- no.
Ev-ery - one
knows
D
Bm
F♯m
ev-ery - thing,
ev-ery - one
knows

ev-ery-thing, no-bo-dy, no-bo-dy has got no-one to go to. The great big no, the great big no, the great big no, the great big no. Whoah!

Lov - er don't turn your head, Lov - er don't turn your head. Lov-er don't turn your head.

Lov-er don't turn your head.

Is no-thing O. - K. with you?

HAND IN MY POCKET

Lyrics by ALANIS MORISSETTE
Music by ALANIS MORISSETTE and GLEN BALLARD

high but I'm ground-ed, I'm sane but I'm o-ver-whelmed, I'm
care but I'm rest-less, I'm here but I'm real-ly gone, I'm
sad but I'm laugh-ing, I'm brave but I'm chick-en shit, I'm

lost but I'm hope-ful, ba-by. What it all comes down
wrong and I'm sor-ry, ba-by. What it all comes down
Solo ends What it all comes down
sick but I'm pret-ty, ba-by. What it all boils down

G5/F   Csus2

to is that ev-'ry-thing's gon-na be
to is that ev-'ry-thing's gon-na be
to is that I have-n't got it all fig-ured
to is that no one's real-ly got it fig-ured

G5

fine, fine, fine. I've got
quite al-right. I've got
out just yet. I've got
out just yet. I've got

one hand in my pock - et and the oth - er one is giv - ing a high five.
one hand in my pock - et and the oth - er one is flick - ing a cig - a - rette.
one hand in my pock - et and the oth - er one is giv - ing the peace sign.
one hand in my pock - et and the oth - er one is play - ing the pi - an - o.

To Coda

I feel

D.S. al Coda

I'm

CODA

And what it all comes down ___ to, my ___ friends, yeah, ___ *is that ev-'ry-thing's just fine, fine, fine.*

I've got one hand in my pock-et and the oth-er one is hail-ing a tax-i-cab.

HOLD ME, THRILL ME, KISS ME, KILL ME
from the Motion Picture BATMAN FOREVER

Lyrics by BONO
Music by U2

Driving Rock

You don't know how you took it, you just know what you got. Oh,

Copyright © 1995 PolyGram International Music Publishing B.V.
All Rights for the United States and Canada Administered by PolyGram International Publishing, Inc.
International Copyright Secured   All Rights Reserved

lawd-y, you been steal-ing from the thieves and you got caught. In the

[A] [G]
head-lights of a stretched car you're a

[E5]
star.

[E5]
Dress-ing like your sis-ter, liv-ing like a tart. If they
don't know how you got here, you just know you want out, be -
want you to be Je-sus, they'll go down on one knee, but they'll

don't know what you're do - in', _____ babe, ___ it must be art. You're a
liev - ing in your - self __ al - most as much as you doubt. You're a
want their mon - ey back if you're a - live ___ at thir - ty three. And you're

head - ache ___ in a suit - case, you're a
big smash ___ you wear it like a rash, you're a
turn - ing tricks __ with your cru - ci - fix, you're a

star. Oh
star. Oh
star. Oh

no, don't be shy. _____ You don't
no, don't be shy. _____ You need
no, don't be shy. _____ You don't

have to go ___ blind. ___
a crowd to ___ cry. ___
have to de-ny your love. ___

Hold ___ me, thrill ___ me, kiss ___ me,

To Coda

kill ___ me.

1.

You

74

D.S. al Coda

They

kill me.

Repeat and Fade

I'LL STICK AROUND

Words and Music by
DAVID GROHL

Medium fast, energetic Rock

Play 4 times

1. I thought I knew all it took to bother you. Every word I said was true. That you'll see.

2. How could it be, I'm the only one who sees your rehearsed insanity,

© 1995 M.J. TWELVE MUSIC
All Rights Controlled and Administered by EMI VIRGIN SONGS, INC.
All Rights Reserved   International Copyright Secured   Used by Permission

77

yeah.

3. I still re- fuse all the meth- ods you a- buse.
4. I've been a- round all the pawns you've gagged and bound.
5., 6. (See additional lyrics)

It's al - right ____ if ____ you're ____ con - fused.
They'll come back ____ and knock ____ you down,

Let me be. ____
and I'll be free. ____

I've tak - en all ____

and I've ____ en - dured. ____

Bb
G
One day it all
C7
will fade, I'm sure.
G5
Eb5
C5
F5
I don't owe you
an - y - thing!
I don't owe you
3 fr

D.S. (with repeats)
G5 Eb5 C5 F5 G5 Eb5 C5 F5
an - y - thing! I don't owe you
G5 Eb5 C5 F5 G5 Eb5 C5 F5
an - y - thing! I don't owe you
G5 Eb5 C5 F5 Eb
an - y - thing! I'll stick a - round,
F G
I'll stick a - round and learn from all

that came from it. I'll stick a-round,

I'll stick a-round and learn from all

that came from it.

Additional Lyrics

5. I had no hand
   In your ever-desperate plan.
   It returns and when it lands,
   Words are due.

6. I should have known
   You were better off alone.
   I looked in and I was shown.
   You were, too.

MOLLY
(SIXTEEN CANDLES)

Words and Music by MIKE CROSS, TIM CROSS,
JOE MAZZOLA, JIM PALUZZI and VINNIE

Fast, bright Rock

See you naked in the bath, cig-a-rette stains on your hands, wilt-ed flow-ers in a vase. I ask, "How

© 1994 EMI Virgin Songs, Inc., It Made A Sound Music and Plunkies Music
All Rights Controlled and Administered by EMI Virgin Songs, Inc.
All Rights Reserved   International Copyright Secured   Used by Permission

are you? Yeah, how are you?"

I see the lip-stick on your
I wipe your back down for a-

glass. I see you're
while. I touch your

drunk I start to laugh.
face you start to smile.

85

I find your note, the letters glare.
Now you know, there's my re - ply.

You say, "I loved you, yeah, I
I wish I loved you, I wish I

loved you."
loved you. Don't ask (Why,

why, don't ask why,) don't ask

sixteen candles down the

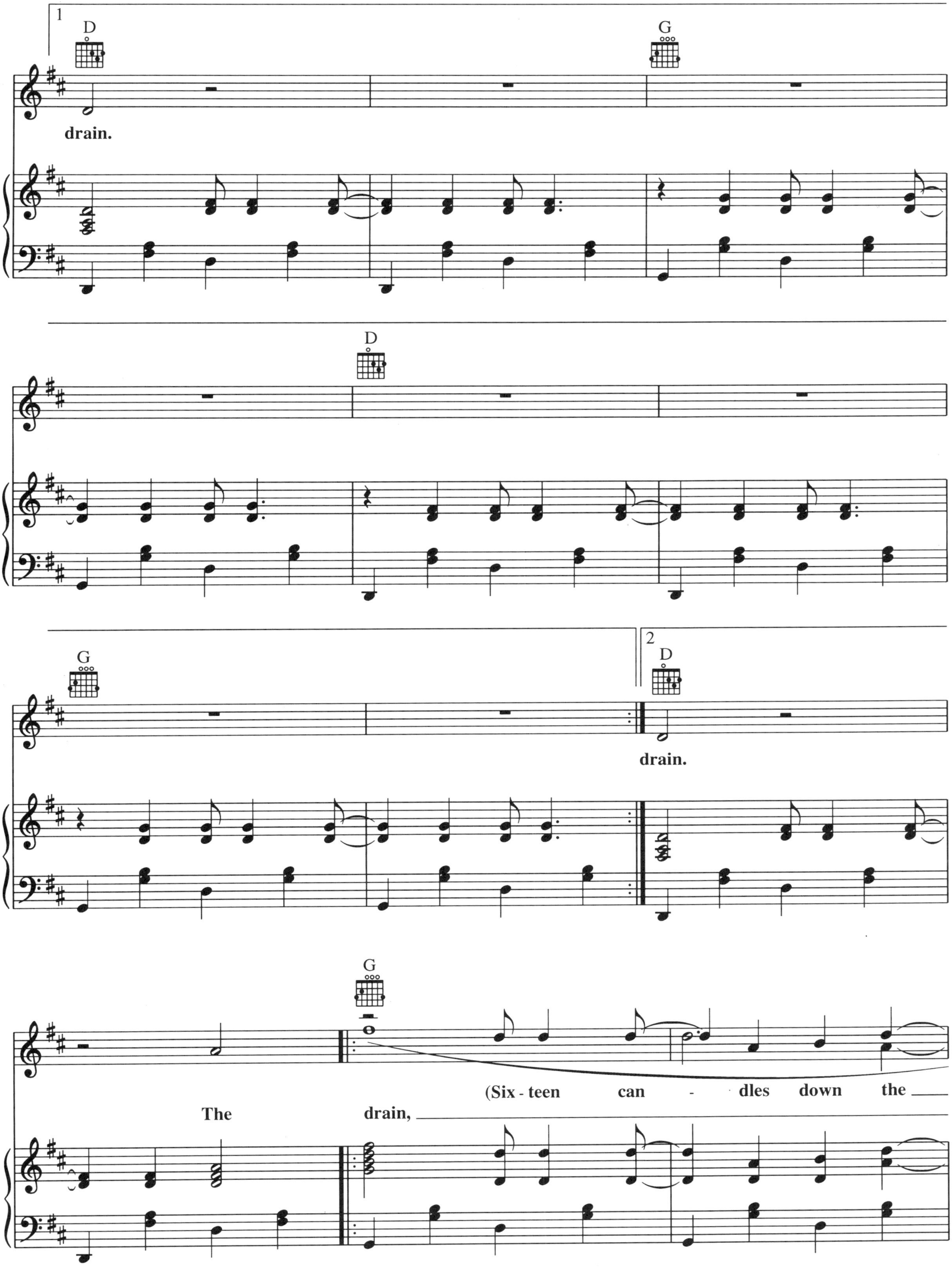
1
D
G
drain.
D
G
2
D
drain.
G
(Six - teen can - dles down the
The drain,

drain.) the drain.

Play 3 times

To Coda

D.S. al Coda
(take 2nd ending)

Don't ask

CODA

Play 4 times

LET HER CRY

Words and Music by DARIUS CARLOS RUCKER, EVERETT DEAN FELBER,
MARK WILLIAM BRYAN and JAMES GEORGE SONEFELD

Moderately slow Rock

She sits a-lone by a lamp-post try'n to find a thought that's es-caped her mind. She says, "Dad's the one I love the most, but Stipe's not far be-hind."

© 1994 EMI APRIL MUSIC INC. and MONICA'S RELUCTANCE TO LOB
All Rights Controlled and Administered by EMI APRIL MUSIC INC.
All Rights Reserved   International Copyright Secured   Used by Permission

G

She nev-er lets me in, ___ on - ly tells __ me where she's _ been ___
This morn-ing I woke up a - lone, ___ found a note _ stand-ing by the phone __
Last night I tried to leave, _ cried so much, _ I could not _ be - lieve

D

C(add9)

when she's had _ too much to drink. _____
say-in', "May-be, may-be I'll be back some day."
she was the same girl I fell in love with long a - go.

G

I say that I don't _ care, ___ I just run my hands through her dark hair, _ and I
I want-ed to look for you, ___ you walked in. I did-n't know just what to do, __ so I
She went in the back _ to ____ get high. I sat down on my couch and cried, _ yell-ing,

D

| C(add9) | G |

pray to God you got-ta help me fly a-way. And just
sat back down, had a beer and felt sor-ry for my-self. Say-in', } let her cry
"Oh, ma-ma, please help me. Won't you hold my hand?" And

| C(add9) | G |

if the tears fall down like rain. Let her sing

| C(add9) | Em G D |

if it eas-es all her pain. Let her go,

| C(add9) | G |

let her walk right out on me. And if the

sun comes up to-mor-row, let her be, ___ { let her be. ___
oh. ___

Let her cry ___

oh, ___ let her be.

MAN IN THE BOX

Lyrics by LAYNE STALEY
Music by JERRY CANTRELL

Moderate Rock

Da da da da da da da da da.

Play 2 times

I'm the man in the box.
I'm the dog who gets beat.

(Guitar Solo ad lib.)

Bur - ied in
Shove my nose

Copyright © 1990 Jack Lord Music and Buttnugget Publishing (ASCAP)
International Copyright Secured   All Rights Reserved

my shit.
in shit. *End Solo*

Won't you come and save me, save me. Feed

G D A
my eyes. (Can you sew them shut?)
Em G D
Je - sus Christ! (De -
A Em G
ny your ma - ker.) He who tries
D A Em
(will be was - ted.) Feed

my eyes. (Now you've sewn them shut.) you've sewn them shut.) Da da da da da da da da da. Da da da da da da da da da.

MAN ON THE MOON

Words and Music by BILL BERRY, PETER BUCK,
MIKE MILLS, MICHAEL STIPE

check-ers and chess.
play Risk.
Yeah, yeah, yeah, yeah.

Mis-ter Fred Blas-sie in a break-fast mess.
See you in heav-en if you make the list.
Yeah, yeah, yeah, yeah.

Hey, An-dy did you hear a-bout this one? Tell me, are you locked in the punch? Hey

Am G C D
An - dy are you goof - ing on El - vis? Hey, ba - by. Are we los - ing touch?
G Am C Bm
If you be - lieved they put a man on the moon,
G Am D G Am
man on the moon. If you be - lieve
C Bm Am
there's noth - ing up my sleeve, then noth - ing is cool.

C
D
C
Mos - es went walk - ing with the staff of wood.
Here's a lit - tle ag - it for the nev - er - be - liev - er.
Yeah, yeah, yeah, yeah.
D
New - ton got beaned by the ap - ple good.
Here's a lit - tle ghost for the of - fer - ing.
C
Yeah, yeah, yeah, yeah.
E - gypt was trou - bled by the
Here's a truck stop in -
D
C
hor - ri - ble asp.
stead of Saint Pe - ter's.
Yeah, yeah, yeah, yeah.

{ Mis-ter Charles Dar-win had the gall to ask.
{ Mis-ter An-dy Kauf-man's gone wres-tl-ing.

Yeah, yeah, yeah, yeah.

Hey An-dy did you hear a-bout this one?

Tell me, are you locked in the punch? Hey An-dy are you goof-ing on El-vis? Hey, ba-by.

{ Are you hav-ing fun?
{ Are we los-ing touch?

| G | Am | C | Bm | G | Am |

If you be-lieved _____ they put a man on the moon, _____ man on the moon. _____

| D | G | Am | C | Bm |

If you be-lieve _____ there's noth-ing up my sleeve, _____

| Am | | Em |

then noth-ing is cool. _____ *Guitar solo*

| D | Em | D | Em |

D
1
2
Solo ends
Solo ends
G
Am
C
Bm
G
Am
If you be - lieved they put a man on the moon, man on the moon.
D
G
Am
C
Bm
If you be - lieve there's noth-ing up my sleeve,
Am
1
2
Em
then noth - ing is cool.

NAME

Gtr. Tuning:
①= E ④= E
②= E ⑤= A
③= A ⑥= D

Words and Music by
JOHN RZEZNIK

Moderately (not too slow)

E - ven though the mo - ment passed me by, I
Scars are sou - ve - nirs you nev - er lose, the
I think a - bout you all the time, but

*This guitar riff is played beginning on the 9th fret.

© 1995 EMI VIRGIN SONGS, INC., FULL VOLUME MUSIC and SCRAP METAL MUSIC
All Rights Controlled and Administered by EMI VIRGIN SONGS, INC.
All Rights Reserved International Copyright Secured Used by Permission

still can't turn a - way.
past is nev - er far.
I don't need the same.

All the dreams you nev -
And did you lose yourself
It's lone - ly where you are.

- er thought you'd lose got tossed a - long the way.
way out there? Did you get to be a star?
Come back down and

Let-ters that you nev-er meant to send
Don't it make you sad to know that life

lost or thrown a-way.
is more than who you are?

Now we're grown up or-phans that nev-er knew their names.
Grew up way too fast and now there's noth-ing to be-lieve.

F♯m7
Esus
We don't be - long _ to no _____ one. That's _ a shame. _
Re - runs all ___ be - come ___ our his - to - ry. _____
Dsus2
F♯m7
If you could hide _ in - side _
A tir - ed song _ keeps play -
Esus
Dsus2
_ me, _ may - be for ___ a - while, _
ing on a tir - ed ra - di - o, _____
and
F♯m7
Esus
Dsus2
I won't _ tell no _____ one ___ your name.

And I won't tell 'em your name.

A/G#
6 fr
Dsus2
5 fr
F#m7
Esus
Dsus2
F#m7
Esus
Instrumental solo - ad lib.
Dsus2
F#m7

111

NEARLY LOST YOU

Featured in the Motion Picture SINGLES

Words and Music by VAN CONNER,
MARK LANEGAN and LEE CONNER

Like the one you knew before,
There's a rider that's fallen and, it's
calling me back once again.
clear there's no time to return.

I nearly,
I nearly,

I nearly lost you there. And it's taking us

somewhere. I nearly lost you there. Well, let's try to see now.

now. *Guitar solo*

115

now. I _____ near-ly lost _____ you _____ there. _____ I _____ near-ly lost _____ you. I _____ near-ly lost _____ you _____ there. _____

F C C7 G
I nearly lost you there.
F C C7 G
I nearly lost you there.
F C C7 G F C
Oh yeah. Oh yeah. Oh
C7 G F C7
Near - ly lost you, babe.
rit.

ODE TO MY FAMILY

Lyrics by DOLORES O'RIORDAN
Music by DOLORES O'RIORDAN and NOEL HOGAN

Moderate rock

Doo, doo, doo, doo; doo, doo, doo, doo; doo, doo, doo; doo, doo, doo, doo; doo, doo, doo, doo.

Copyright © 1994 Island Music Ltd.
All Rights for the U.S. and Canada Administered by Songs Of PolyGram International, Inc.
International Copyright Secured   All Rights Reserved

Gsus2
A7sus
D
Bm
Un - der - stand the things I
Un - der - stand what I've be -
F♯m
Gsus2
A7sus
say, don't turn a - way from me,
come, it was - n't my de - sign.
D
Bm
'cause I spent half my life out
And peo - ple ev - 'ry - where think
F♯m
Gsus2
A7sus
there, you would - n't dis - a - gree.
some - thing bet - ter than I am.

| D | Bm |

Do you see ___ me? Do you see? ___ Do you like ___
But I miss ___ you, I miss, ___ 'cause I liked ___

| F#m | Gsus2 | A7sus |

___ me? Do you like ___ me stand - ing there?
___ it, 'cause I liked ___ it, when I was out there.

| D | Bm |

Do you no - tice? Do you know? ___ Do you see ___
Do you know ___ this? Do you know ___ you did not

| F#m | Gsus2 | A7sus |

___ me? Do you see ___ me? Does an - y - one care?
find me. You did not ___ find. Does an - y - one care?

D
Bm
F♯m
Un-hap - pi-ness where's when I was young and we
Gsus2
A7sus
D
Bm
did-n't give a damn, 'cause we were raised to see life
F♯m
Gsus2
A7sus
D
as fun and take it if we can. My moth - er,
Bm
F♯m
Gsus2
A7sus
my moth - er, she hold me, she hold me when I was out there.

My fa-ther, my fa-ther, he liked me, oh, he liked me. Does an-y-one care?

me. Does an-y-one care?

Does an-y-one care? Does an-y-one care? Does an-y-one care?

1
Gsus2
A7sus
2
Gsus2
A7sus
D
Does an-y-one care?
Doo, doo, doo, doo; doo,
Bm
F♯m
1,2
Gsus2
A7sus
doo, doo, doo; doo, doo, doo, doo; doo, doo, doo, doo; doo,
3
Gsus2
A7sus
D
Bm
doo, doo, doo.
F♯m
Gsus2
A7sus
D

SCUM

Words and Music by
CURT KIRKWOOD

In some for-get-ta-ble rhyme we crawled a-cross the bor-der-line.
I thought a beau-ti-ful thing. A fire was lit with-in my mind.

We kissed the en-e-my till I thought we tra-veled out of time.
On ru-by hum-ming-bird wings went shiver-ing up and down my spine.

You could-n't have heard me speak. There was, so it did seem, I say,
The wa-ter that quit our thirst was not from earth-ly vine-yards mined.

a fog so hea-vy that I could not tell it was night or day.
And then we drunk-en-ly sailed the gut-ter of our in-vis-i-ble shrine.

Hand over all water. You know that means business, scum. Under the stone, we find the scum. Under the stars, we find ___ the scum.

Instrumental Solo

Play 4 times

D.S. al Coda (2nd verse)

CODA

Play 4 times

SICK OF MYSELF

Words and Music by
MATTHEW SWEET

Medium Rock

You don't know how you move me, de-con-struct me, and all you take of me, e-ven room to breathe, the choice consume me. I'm all used up, I'm out to leave you. All to throw a-way a chance

© 1995 EMI BLACKWOOD MUSIC INC. and CHARM TRAP MUSIC INC.
All Rights Controlled and Administered by EMI BLACKWOOD MUSIC INC.
All Rights Reserved   International Copyright Secured   Used by Permission

[C] [G] [F] [C] [G] [F] [C]

__ of luck,_ I am __ star - struck _ by some - thing in __ your eyes __
__ at great - ness, just __ to make _ this dream _ come in - to play._

[G] [F] [C]

__ that is keep - ing my hope _ a - live. __ But I'm sick of my -
__ I don't know __ if I'll find _ a way, __ 'cause I'm

[F] [G] [C]

self when I look at you, ____ some-thing as beau - ti - ful __ and true. _

[F] [G]

__ World that's ug - ly and a lie, _____ it's hard to e -

-ven want to try. I'm be-gin-ning to think may-be you don't know.

I'm be-gin-ning to think may-be you don't know.

131

STARS

Written by JEFF DIMPSEY, TIM LASH,
BRYAN ST. PERE and MATT TALBOT

Moderately slow

She thinks she missed the train to Mars; she's out back counting stars.

She thinks she missed the train to Mars; she's out back counting

Copyright © 1995 by Careers-BMG Music Publishing, Inc. and Martians Go Home Music
All Rights Administered by Careers-BMG Music Publishing, Inc.
International Copyright Secured   All Rights Reserved

stars.

She's not at work, she's not in school,
I found her out back sitting nak-

she's not in bed. I think I've fin - 'lly broke her.
ed, look-ing up and look - ing dead.

I bring her on home with ev - 'ry-thing I want
A crum - pled yel - low piece of pa -

per, noth-ing that she needs.
sev - en nines and tens.

(1.,2.) I thought she'd be there hold - ing dais -
(D.S.) I thought you'd be there hold - ing dais -

-ies, she always waits for me.
-ies, you always wait for me.

She thinks she missed the train to Mars; she's out back counting stars.

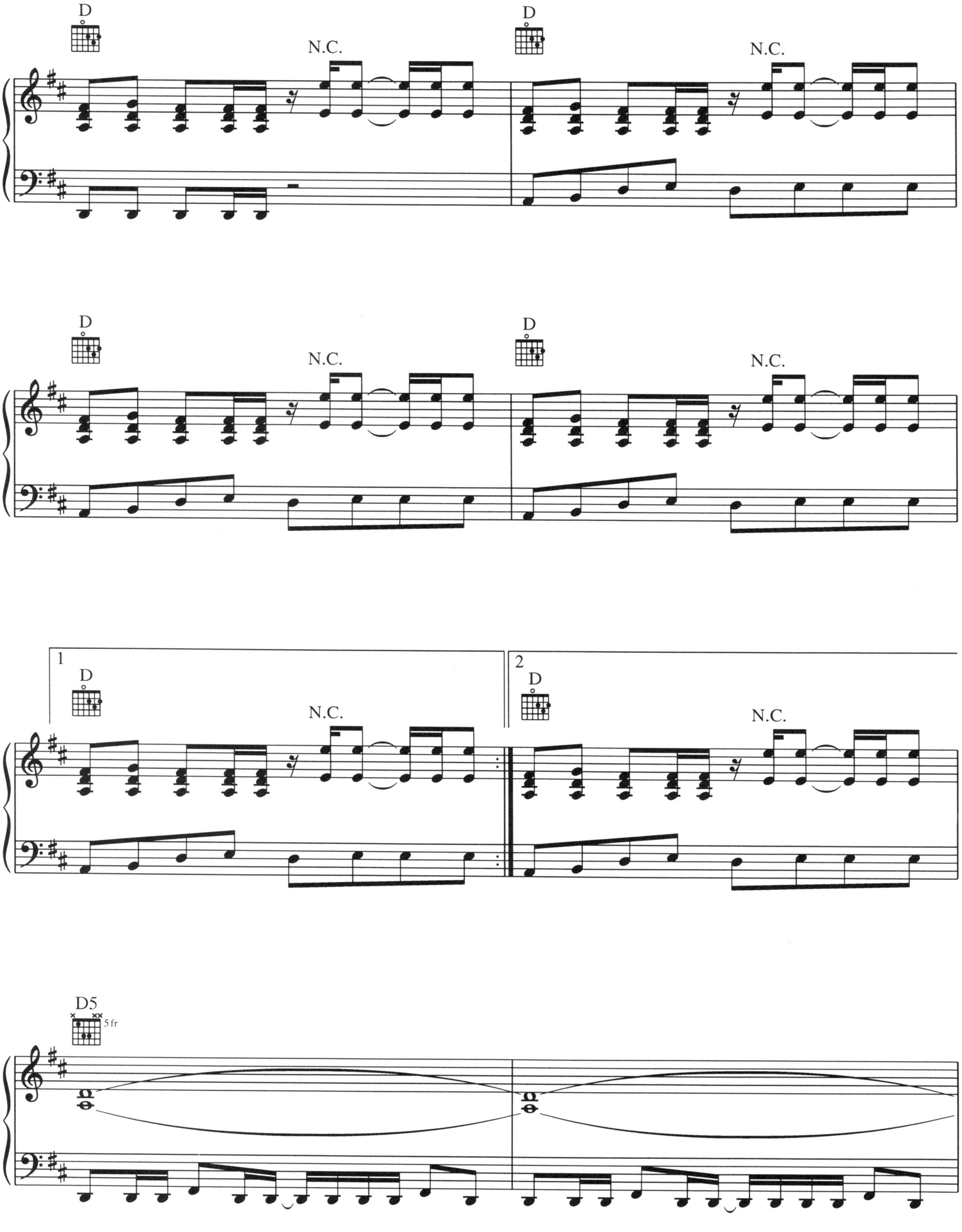
D
N.C.
D
N.C.
D
N.C.
D
N.C.
1
D
N.C.
2
D
N.C.
D5
5 fr

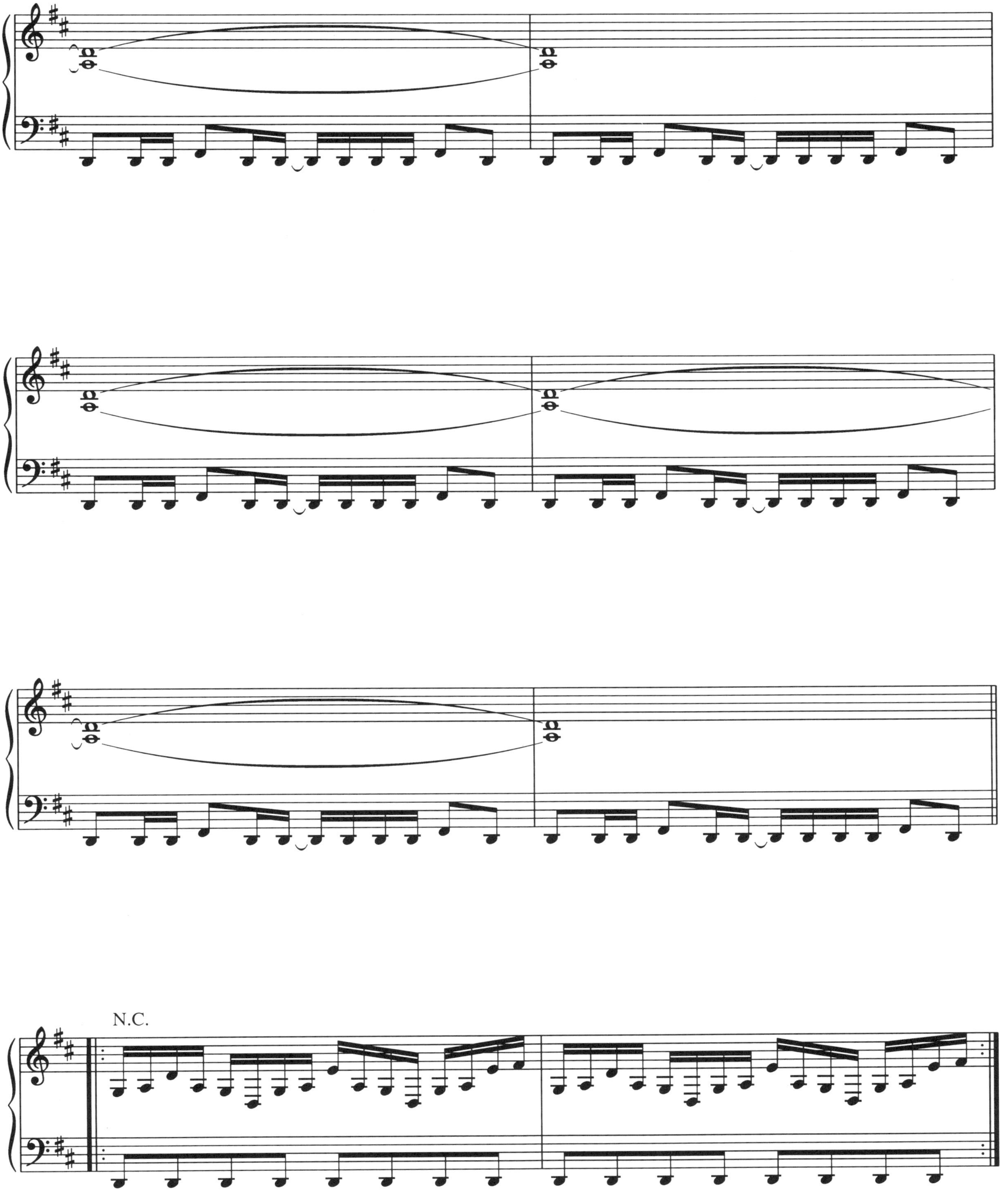
N.C.

stars.

RIGHT HERE, RIGHT NOW

Words and Music by
JESUS JONES

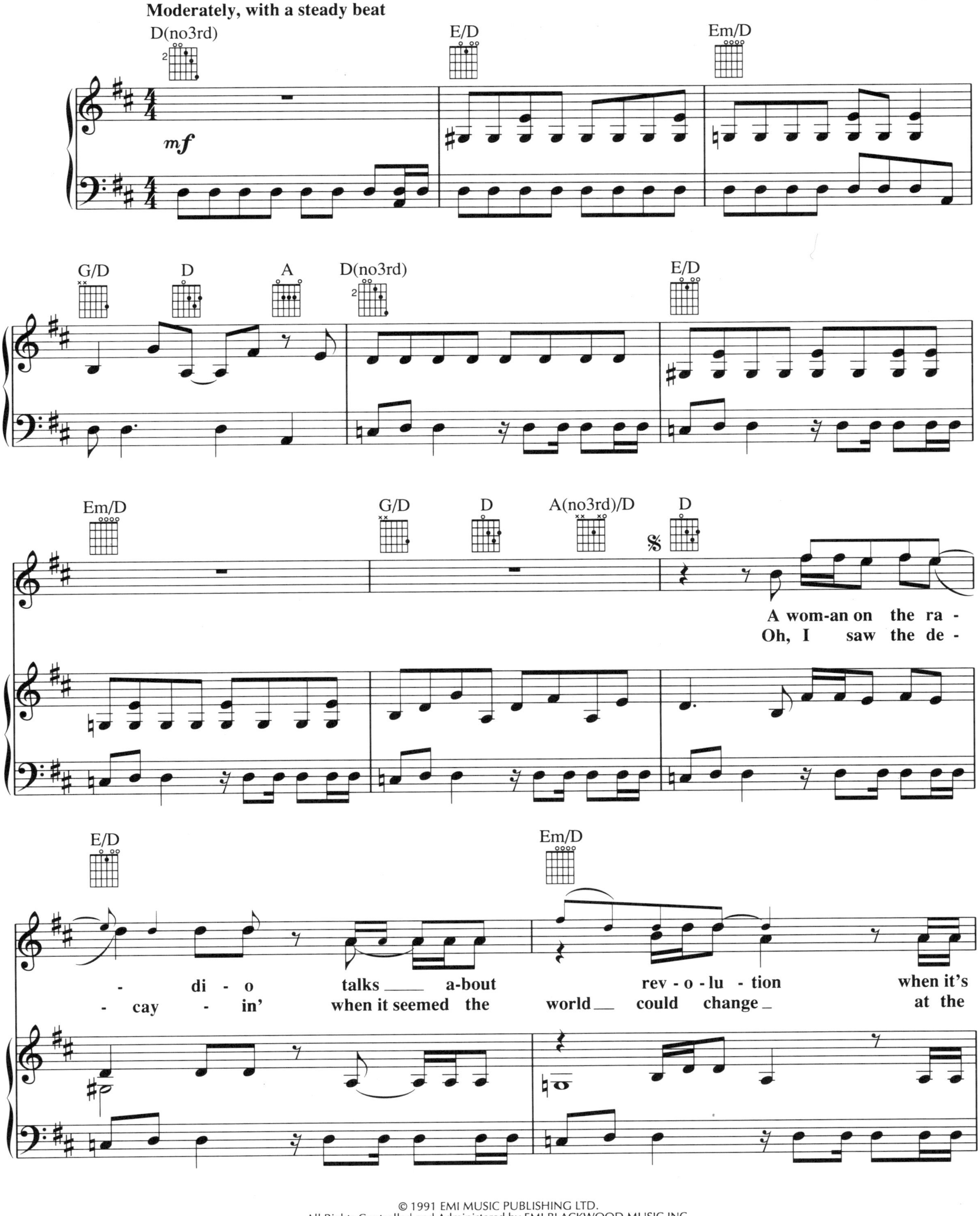

G/D
D
A(no3rd)/D
D
al - read - y passed her by. Bob Dyl - an de - nied
blink of an eye. And if an -
E/D
Em/D
this to sing a - bout. You know, it feels good to be
y - thing, then there's your sound
G/D
D
A/D
G
a - live.
of the times.
I was a - live and I wait -
- ed, wait - ed.
I was a - live and I wait -

-ed for this. Right here, right now, there is no other place I wanna be. Right here, right now watching the world wake up from his-to-ry.

D.S. al Coda

CODA

Right here, right now.

Guitar solo ad lib.

Play 4 times

I was a-live___ and I wait - ed, wait - ed.

I was a-live___ and I wait - ed___ for ___ this.

Right ___ here, right ___ now, _____ there is no oth -

er place I ____ wan - na be. Right ____ here, right ____ now, _____ watch - ing the world ____ wake up ____ from his - to - ry. wake up.

STARSEED

Words and Music by MICHAEL TURNER, MICHAEL "RAINE" MAIDA, CHRIS EACRETT and ARNOLD LANNI

Moderately fast Rock

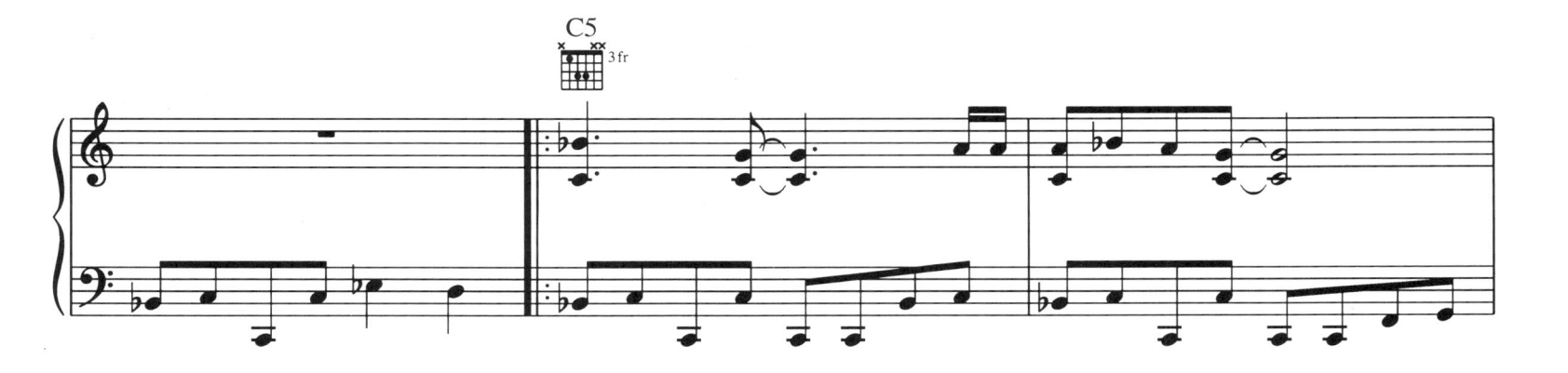

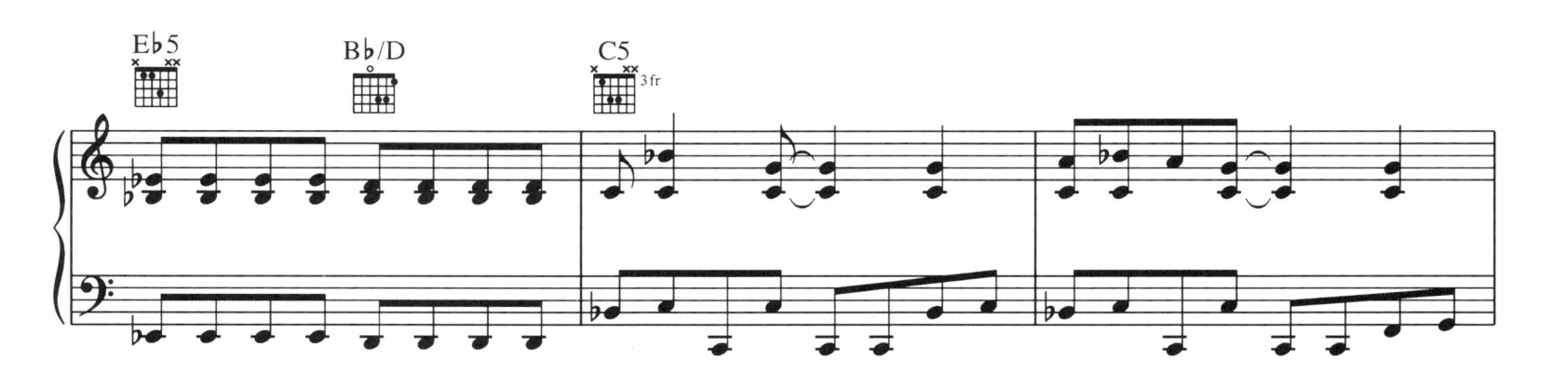

Copyright © 1994 Sony/ATV Tunes LLC, Under Zenith Publishing, Seacret Publishing, Catchit Songs and Lanni Tunes
All Rights on behalf of Sony/ATV Tunes LLC, Under Zenith Publishing, Seacret Publishing and Catchit Songs
Administered by Sony/ATV Music Publishing, 8 Music Square West, Nashville, TN 37203
International Copyright Secured   All Rights Reserved

I let go of the world that was holding a
I hoped to find why the world wasn't glowing; it's

pas - sen - ger that could not fly. In
dark - er as we end this ride. I've

search of souls, in search of some - thing.
fall - en back under the e - qua - tor.

Let it go, let it slide.
I'm back in - side, we're back in - side.
F5
Eb5
Bb/D
Yeah, yeah, yeah, yeah, yeah,
C5
Oh,

yeah, ___ yeah, ___ yeah, ___ yeah. ___

When I find out ___ what ___ went on, ___ we'll bring it back ___ but it won't ___ be eas-y. They won't be-lieve ___ how a man, ___

he could drown in a star-seed, star-seed.

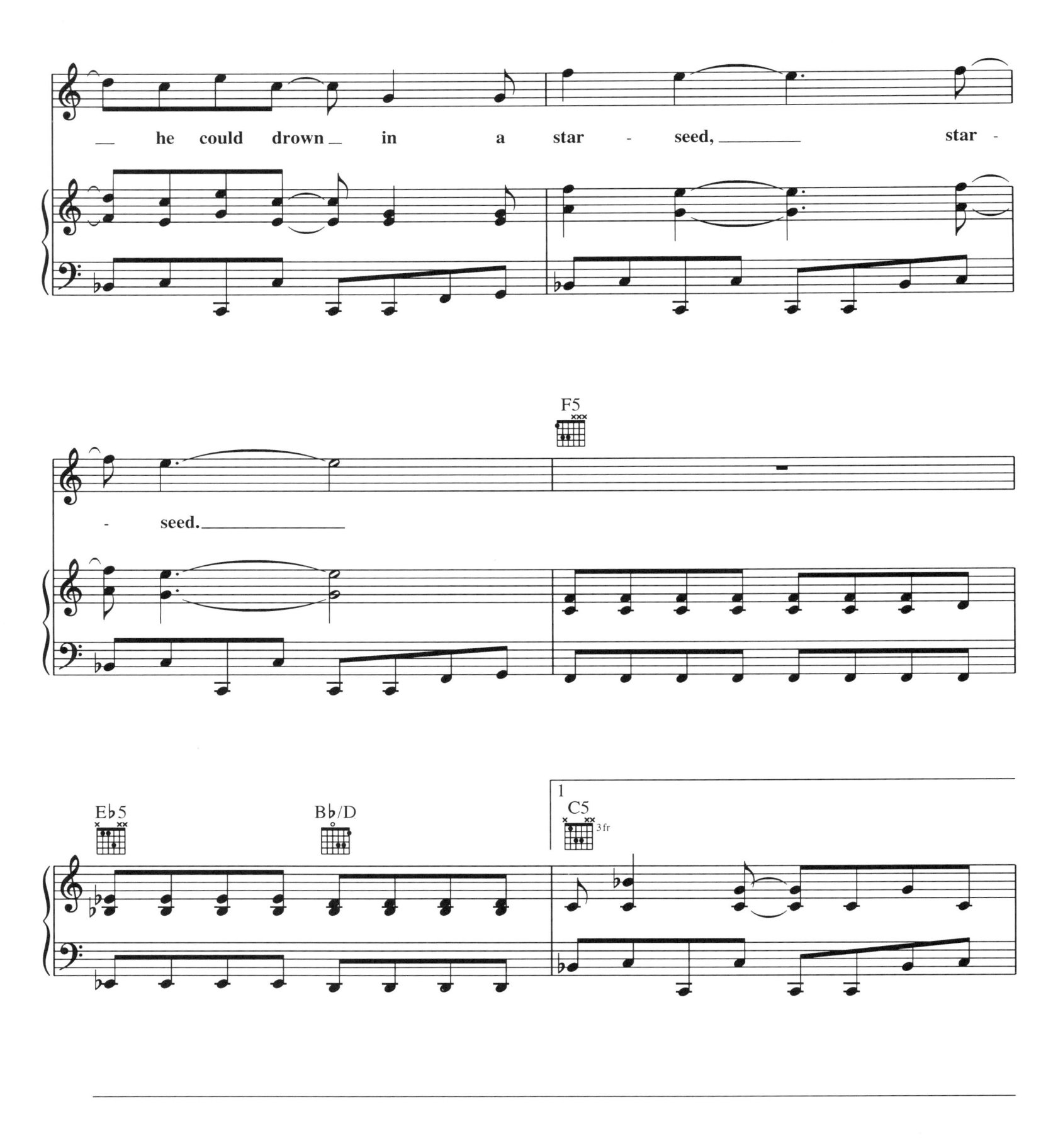

149

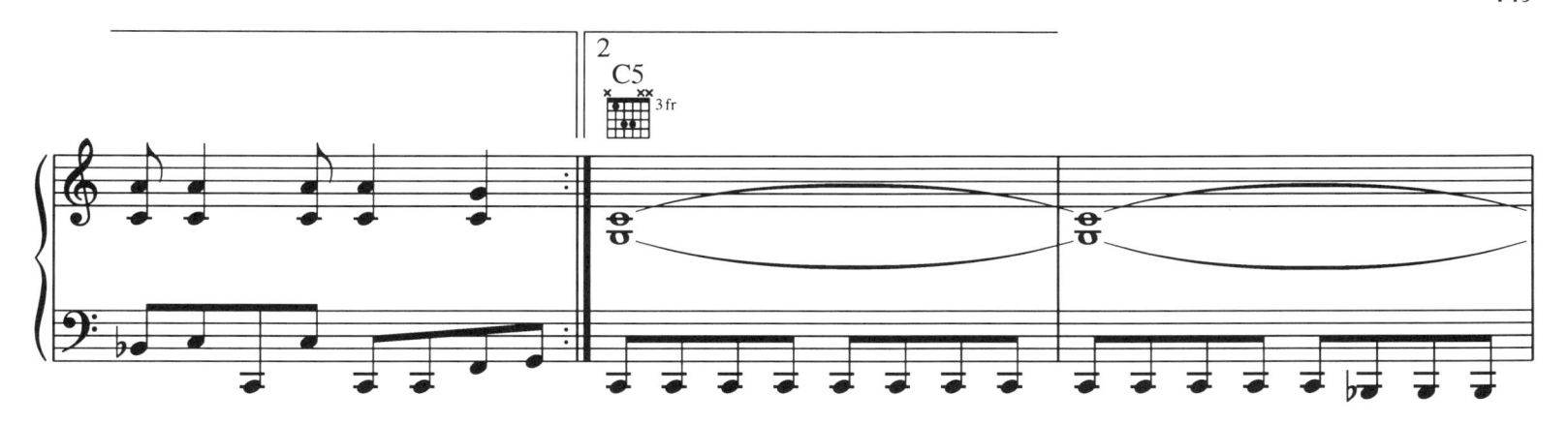

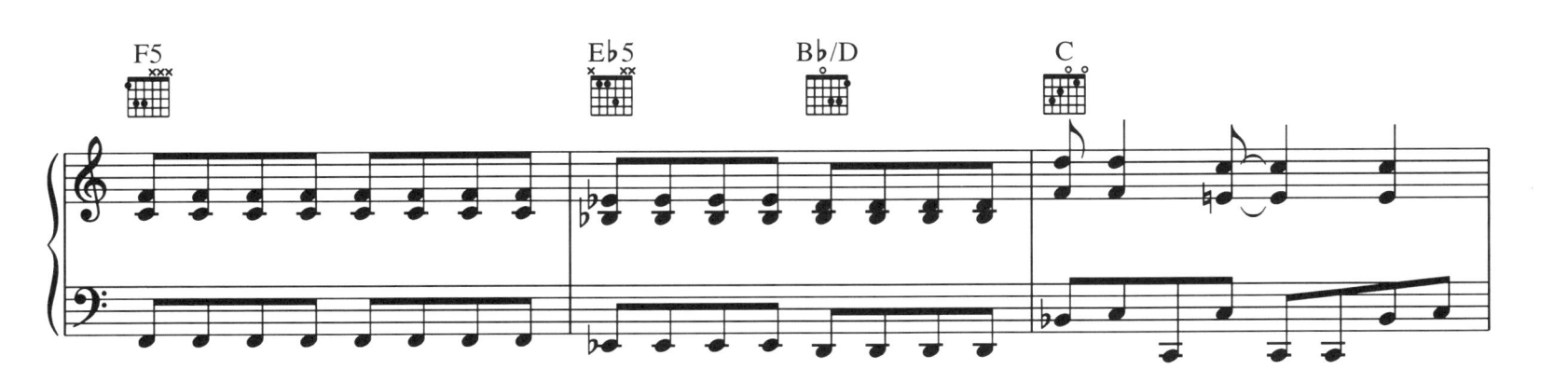

Solo ends **Nothing, nothing. But I found out what went on, we'll bring it back but it won't be easy. They won't believe the man, he could, but I'd choose starseed over nothing, nothing. When I —ing, nothing.**

Star - seed o - ver, star - seed o - ver.

STUTTER

Words and Music by
JUSTINE FRISCHMANN

Fast Rock

No need to whine, boy, like a wind up toy, you stutter at my feet.
Don't feed me a line, boy, I can hear that voice you use up on the phone.
And it's never the time, boy, you've had too much wine to
And there's no need to be coy, that is something you can

© 1993 EMI Music Publishing Ltd.
All Rights Controlled and Administered by EMI Blackwood Music Inc.
All Rights Reserved International Copyright Secured Used by Permission

stum-ble up my street. Well, it is-n't a prob - lem,
do up - on your own. Well, it is-n't a prob - lem,

noth-ing we can't keep be - tween the sheets. Tell me you're mine,
noth-ing we can't solve, so just re - lax. Am I on the right train,

love, and I will not wait for oth - er bed - time
love, and will I have to tie you to the

treats.
tracks?

Is there some-thing you lack

D5
5 fr
F5
C5
3 fr
when I'm flat on my back? Is there some-thing that I can do for you?
G5
3 fr
D5
5 fr
F5
It's al-ways some-thing you ate, or it's some-thing you hate. Tell me, is it the way
C5
3 fr
G5
3 fr
D5
5 fr
that I touch you? Have you found a new mate and is she real-ly great?
F5
C5
3 fr
E♭5
Is it just that I'm much, too much for you, oh,

oh?

I real-ly want you to, _____ oh, _____ oh. _____

I real-ly want you to, oh, _____ oh. _____

SUPERNOVA

Words and Music by
LIZ PHAIR

Moderate Rock

I have looked all o-ver the place, but you have got my fa-vor-ite face. Your eye-lash-es spar-kle like

You walk in clouds of glit-ter and the sun re-flects your eyes, and ev-'ry time the wind blows, I can smell you in the sky. Your kiss-es are as wick-ed as an

Copyright © 1994 Sony/ATV Tunes LLC and Civil War Days Music
All Rights Administered by Sony/ATV Music Publishing, 8 Music Square West, Nashville, TN 37203
International Copyright Secured   All Rights Reserved

gild - ed grass and your lips __ are sweet _ and slip - p'ry like _ a sher-
M six - teen, and you fought _ like a __ vol - ca - no _ and you're ev-

-iff's bare _ red ass. __
-'ry - thing _ to me. __

'Cause you're a hu - man su - per - no - va, a so - lar su - per - man. _ You're an an - gel with wings _ of fire, __ a fly - ing gi - ant fric - tion _ blast. __

2
D5
5 fr
E5
C5
3 fr
D5
5 fr
- tion _ blast. _ You're a fly - ing gi - ant fric - tion _ blast. ___
N.C.
E5
D.S. al Coda
Guitar Solo
Solo Ends
'Cause you're a
CODA
D5
5 fr
N.C.
- tion __ blast. ____
E5
1-3
4

TRIGGER HAPPY JACK
(DRIVE BY A GO-GO)

Words and Music by POE
and JEFFREY CONNOR

Moderately

He scares eas-i-ly; __ it makes him so __ an-gry at me. __ And his head spins a-round just like the Ex-or-cist, and I find it ev-er so hard to re-sist __ his cries. 1. But there's

Copyright © 1995 Sony/ATV Songs LLC, Apro Poe Go Music and Connor Skerrett Music
All Rights on behalf of Sony/ATV Songs LLC and Apro Poe Go Music Administered by Sony/ATV Music Publishing, 8 Music Square West, Nashville TN 37203
International Copyright Secured   All Rights Reserved

nothing more sadistic than an infant waving his pistol in my face. He wants me right down on my knees, *crumbling in disgrace.* But he underestimates my mind. I know he's messing with my head. My only weakness is I can't believe the guy could be entirely dead. You

2., 3. *(See additional lyrics)*

can't talk to a psy-cho like a nor-mal hu-man be-ing. You can't talk to a psy-cho like a nor-mal hu-man be-ing. Trig-ger hap-py Jack, you're gon-na blow, but I'm gon-na get off be-fore you go! My trig-ger hap-py Jack is just a drive by, a go-go. Go-go.

Csus C Ab+(sus2) Csus C Ab+(sus2) Csus C Ab+(sus2) Ab/Bb Bb
3fr 3fr 3fr 3fr 3fr 3fr
2
Chorus
N.C. Gb5 N.C.
a go - go. Why do you make me feel like this?
Ab5 Gb5
4fr
Why do you got-ta be such a dick? Why do you make me feel like
N.C. Ab5 N.C. Bb5 B5
4fr
this? Why do you got-ta be __ such a dick? Go - go.

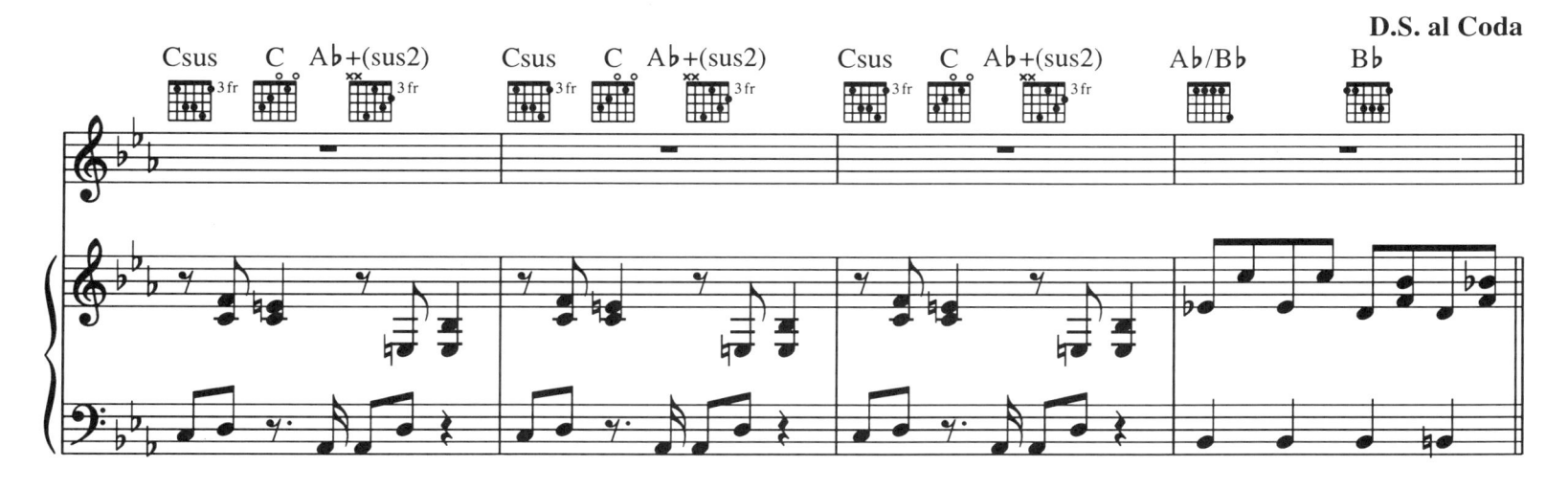

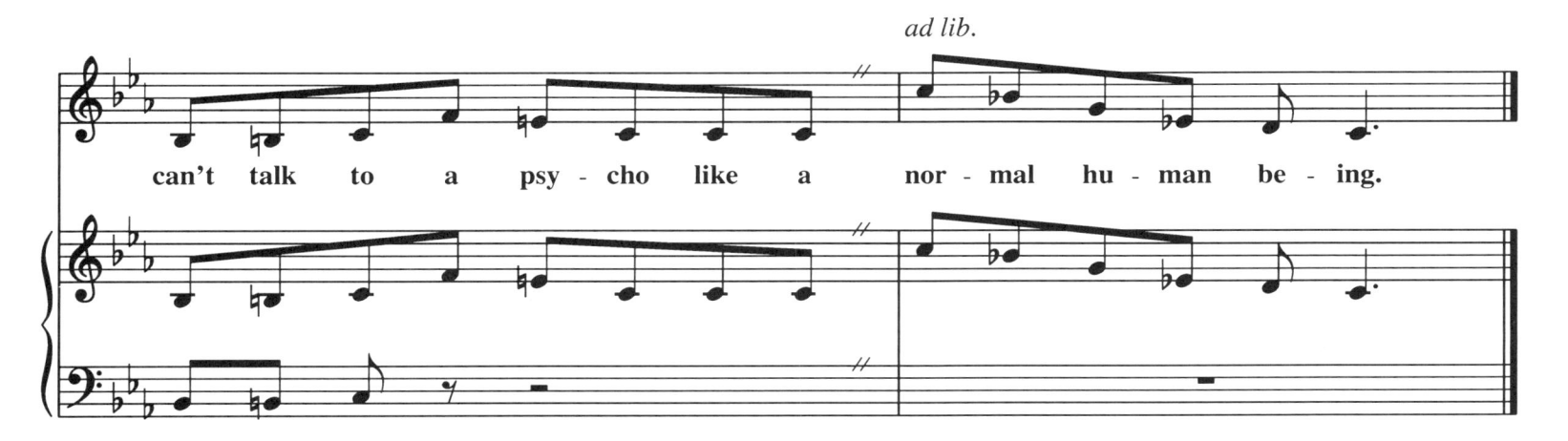

Additional Lyrics

2. And after awhile he calms down
   And he looks at me like a prince
   But I know I better bite the bullet
   'Cause it's just another one of his
   Jedi mind tricks

   Well this ain't no headtrip honey
   This is a collision on the road
   And you've got me feeling oh just like a road kill
   but you know deep down I know

   To Chorus:

3. And I hate myself
   Just enough to want him
   But I hate him just enough to get off

   But I understand him
   Maybe I'm just crazy enough
   To love him
   Why not?

   To Chorus:

TWO PRINCES

Words and Music by
SPIN DOCTORS

Moderately fast

One, two princes kneel before you. (That's what I said, now.)
This one, he got a princely rack-et. (That's what I said, now.)

Princes, princes who adore you. (Just go ahead, now.)
Got some big seal upon his jacket (ain't in his head, now.)

Copyright © 1991 Sony/ATV Songs LLC and Mow B'Jow Music
All Rights Administered by Sony/ATV Music Publishing, 8 Music Square West, Nashville, TN 37203
International Copyright Secured   All Rights Reserved

One has diamonds in __ his pockets (that's some bread, __ now.)
Marry him, your father will __ condone __ you. (How 'bout that, __ now.) You

This one, he wants to buy __ you rockets, (ain't in his head, __ now.)
marry me, your father will __ disown __ you. (He'll eat his hat, __ now.)

Yeah, _____ yeah, yeah. _____ (Di di ba

dip. Di dip dip di dip. Ba dee-dle-ee di ba du ba du ba du ba du ba du ba du ba du ba.)

Mar-ry him or mar-ry me. I'm ___ the one that loves you, ba-by. Can't you see? Ain't got no fu-ture or a fam-'ly tree, ___ but I know what a prince and lov-er ought to be. ___ I know what a prince and lov-er ought to be. ___ Said, If you want to call ___ me, ba- by, (just go a-head, ___ now.) And if you want to tell ___ me may-be, (just go a-head, ___ now.) And if you wanna buy me flowers, (just go ahead, now.) And if you want to talk for hours, (just go ahead, now.)

1. *Instrumental solo*
2. one, two princes kneel before you. (That's what I said, now.) Princes, princes who adore you. (Just go ahead, now.) One has diamonds in his pock-

-ets (and that's some bread, now.) This one, he wants to buy you rock-

-ets, (ain't in his head, now.) Mar-ry him or mar-ry me. I'm

the one that loves you, ba-by. Can't you see? I ain't got no fu-ture or a fam-'ly tree, but

Solo ends **Said**

I know what a prince and lov-er ought to be. I know what a prince and lov-er ought to be.

Said if you want to call me, ba-by, (just go a-head, now.) And if you want to tell me may-be, (just go a-head, now.) And if you wan-na buy me flow-ers, (just go a-head, now.) And if you want to talk for hours, (just go a-head, now.) And

Repeat ad lib. and Fade

UNDONE - THE SWEATER SONG

Words and Music by
RIVERS CUOMO

Moderately slow Rock

I'm me, me be, God damn, I am. I can sing and
Oh no, it go, it gone, bye-bye. Who I, I think,

hear me, know me.
I sink, and I die. } If you want to de-stroy my sweat-er,

hold this thread as I walk a-way.

Copyright © 1994 E.O. Smith Music
International Copyright Secured   All Rights Reserved

Watch me un-rav-el, I'll soon be nak-ed.

Ly-in' on the floor, I've come un-done.

Guitar Solo

Solo Ends

If you want to destroy my sweater, __ hold this thread as I walk a-way __ Watch me un-rav-el, I'll soon be nak-ed. Ly-in' on the floor, I've come un-done. __ come un-done. __

G C D C
Play 4 times
G C
Guitar Solo
Ooh, ooh
(Solo continues to end.)
D C G C D C
ooh, ooh. Ooh, ooh, ooh, ooh.
G C D C
Ooh, ooh, ooh, ooh.
G C D C G
Ooh, ooh, ooh, ooh, ooh.

WHAT'S UP

Words and Music by
LINDA PERRY

Slowly

Twen-ty-five years of my life and still I'm trying to get up that great big hill of hope for a des-ti-na-

And I try, oh my God, do I try, I try all the time in this in-sti-tu-

Copyright © 1992 by Stuck In The Throat Music and Famous Music Corporation
International Copyright Secured   All Rights Reserved

A
- tion. I real-ize quick - ly when I
- tion. And I pray,
Bm
know I should, _ that the world _ was made up of this broth-er - hood _ of
oh my God, __ do I pray, __ I pray ev - 'ry sin-gle
D
A
man, for what-ev - er that means. _
day for a rev - o - lu - tion. __
And so I cry some-times when I'm ly - in' in bed __ just to

get it all out, _ what's in ____ my head, _ and I, I am feeling a little pe-cu-liar. And so I wake in the morn-ing and I step out-side, _ and I take a deep breath, _ and I get _ real high, _ and I scream from the top of my lungs, _ "What's go-in' on?" _

And I ___ say, "Hey, ___ hey." ___ I said, "Hey, ___ what's goin' on?" ___ And I ___ say, "Hey, ___ hey." ___

D
To Coda
I said, "Hey,
what's go - in' on?"
A
1.
D.C.
(with repeats)
2.
D.S. al Coda
And I say,
CODA
A
Ooh,
ooh,
Bm
ooh,

D
ooh, uh-huh.
rit.
Slower, easy shuffle
A
Twen-ty-five years of my
Bm
life and still I'm trying to get up that great big hill of hope
D
A
for a des-ti-na-tion.
rit.

WONDERWALL

Words and Music by
NOEL GALLAGHER

♩=90

To-day is gon-na be the day that they're gon-na throw it back to you,
by now you should-'ve some-how re-al-ised what you got-ta do.

Copyright © 1995 Sony Music Publishing United Kingdom and Creation Songs Ltd.
All Rights Administered by Sony/ATV Music Publishing, 8 Music Square West, Nashville, TN 37203
International Copyright Secured   All Rights Reserved

F♯m
A
Esus4
F♯m
I don't be - lieve that an - y - bo - dy feels the way I do a - bout you now.
Dmaj7
Esus4
F♯m
F♯m
A
Esus4
Bm
1. Back - beat the word was on the street that the fi - re in your heart is out.
(Verse 2 see block lyric)
F♯m
A
Esus4
Bm
I'm sure you've heard it all be - fore but you nev - er real - ly had a doubt.

I don't believe that anybody feels the way I do about you now.

And all the roads we have to walk are winding and all the lights that lead us there are blinding.

D
E
A
/G♯
F♯m
There are ma - ny things that I would like to say to you but I don't know how,
Bm
be - cause
I said
D
F♯m
A
F♯m
may - be
you're gon - na be the one that
D
F♯m
A
F♯m
D
F♯m
saves me,
and af - ter all

you're my won-der-wall.

I said may-be you're gon-na be the one that saves me, and af-ter all you're my won-der-wall. I said may - be _____ you're gon - na be the one that saves me, _____ you're gon - na be the one that

(Continue as instr.)

Repeat 7 times

Verse 2:
Today was gonna be the day
But they'll never throw it back to you
By now you should've somehow
Realised what you're not to do
I don't believe that anybody
Feels the way I do
About you now.

And all the roads that lead you there were winding
And all the lights that light the way are blinding
There are many things that I would like to say to you
But I don't know how.

UNDER THE BRIDGE

Words and Music by ANTHONY KIEDIS, FLEA, CHAD SMITH and JOHN FRUSCIANTE

Slow Rock ballad

Some-times I feel ___ like I don't have a part- ner.
drive on her streets ___ 'cause she's my com-pan- ion. I
hard to be-lieve ___ that there's no-bod-y out ___ there. It's

Some-times I feel ___ like I
walk through her hills 'cause she
hard to be-lieve ___ that

© 1991 EMI Blackwood Music Inc. and MOEBETOBLAME MUSIC
All Rights Controlled and Administered by EMI Blackwood Music Inc.
All Rights Reserved International Copyright Secured Used by Permission

my on - ly friend ___ is the cit - y I live ___ in, the
knows who I am. ___ She sees my good deeds ___ and she
I'm all a - lone. ___ At least I have her ___ love, the

cit - y of an - gels. Lone - ly as I ___ am, to -
kiss - es me wind - y. I nev - er wor - ry. Now,
cit - y, she loves ___ me. Lone - ly as I ___ am, to -

geth - er we cry. ___
that is a lie. ___
geth - er we cry. ___

I

I don't ev - er want to feel _____ like I did that day.

Take me to the place I love, _____ take me all the way.

I don't ev-er want to feel _____ like I did that day.

To Coda

Take me to the place I love, _____ take me all the way, _____ yeah, _____ yeah, yeah. _____

D.S. al Coda (Take 2nd ending)

It's

CODA

_take me all the way, ___ yeah, ___ yeah, ___ yeah. ___

Oh, ___ no ___ no no, ___ yeah, ___ yeah. ___

Love me, ___ I said, ___ yeah, ___ yeah. ___

One time.   Un-der the bridge down-town

is where I drew some blood. Un-der the bridge down-town

I could not get e-nough. Un-der the bridge down-town

for-got a-bout my love. Un-der the bridge down-town

I gave my life a-way. *Vocal ad lib.*

Play 8 times

last time - rit.